For

BY
LOUISE WOLLMAN

DESIGN
BY JANE WILSON

PETER PAUPER PRESS, INC.
WHITE PLAINS • NEW YORK

To the many Grand-People in my life: my honey, my children, my Mom, my incredible, supportive friends

Peter Pauper Press, Inc.
202 Mamaroneck Avenue
White Plains, NY 10601
ISBN 0-88088-211-5
Library of Congress No. 89-63622
Printed in Hong Kong
7 6 5 4 3 2

CONTENTS

THAT OLD GRANDMERE—SHE AIN'T
WHAT SHE USED TO BE! 5

GRANNIES OF MINIMUM AGE
MAKE MAXIMUM WAGE 9

YOUR GRANDMOTHER WEARS
COMBAT BOOTS! 14

THERE'LL BE A HOT TIME IN
THE OLD GOWN TONIGHT! 20

SEX CHANGES 25

GOODNESS GRACIOUS,
GREAT GRAM'S A FLYER! 28

GRANNY, GET YOUR GUN! 33

GRANDMOTHER, WHAT BIG
THIGHS YOU HAVE! 36

WEIGHTY GRANNECDOTES 40

THE OTHER WOMAN 42

THE "GRAMMIE" AWARDS 46

ANYTHING YOU CAN SAY,
I CAN SAY BETTER! 50

YOU'RE A GRAND OLD BAG!
In Grandchildren's Own Words 57

THAT OLD GRANDMERE

SHE AIN'T WHAT SHE USED TO BE!

THAT OLD GRANDMERE—SHE AIN'T WHAT SHE USED TO BE!

Once upon a time and not so very long ago, a grandmother was a little old lady who dressed in a print housedress and sensible lace-up shoes, fluttered around her kitchen, kneading dough and rolling pie crusts, kept her knitting close at hand, hummed hymns while nodding off in front of the hearth—and was always available to babysit the grandkids.

Well, that olden days grandma, so quaint and saintly, simply ain't no more. Today's grandma, if she's still into carrots, probably spells it "karats." Say "Grams" and she'll give you her Weight Watchers count for the day. Remember her fondly but don't expect to find her at home to fondle you.

Although you won't often find today's grandmother in the kitchen (unless she's Julia Child), she still wields a mean whisk, knows her way around a wok, and is fluent in microwave. Grandma hasn't forgotten how to make pot roast, but is more apt to be found poaching fish in a dill/cilantro/sorrel broth.

The old-style grandmother watched YOUR weight—today's Granny watches HERS. Yesterday's had wicker in her cellar; today's has wine.

Most people remember their grandmother with a cup of coffee in the kitchen. Kids today find Grandma with a Diet Coke in front of the dresser. Yesteryear's design grandmother pushed her hair into a bun, donned her glasses and was off to milk the cow; today's Designer Grandmother puts on her pancake, fluffs her perm, pops in her contacts and is off to the office. Grammie of the past spoke of cookies and compresses; "Now Nanas" are conversant in computers.

Expect grandma to be wearing lamé, not lace; a jumpsuit, not a jumper; polyester, not petticoats; and sneakers instead of support hose. Her skin may be as wrinkle-free as a drip-dry dress, due either to the kindness of Nature or to the miracles of Modern Medicine (only her plastic surgeon knows for sure).

Though she's got a whole new look and style, our 1990's Nana hasn't changed much on the inside. The original inspiration for the cheerleader, she loves her grandchildren fiercely and defends them against all critics, especially their parents.

There's a place in her heart that did not exist until her grandchildren were born and thereafter will never be occupied by anyone else. And there's a place in her wallet that is stuffed with photos of her adored grandchildren.

She used to be called Alice, Agnes, or Rose. Now she's Jackie, Barbara or Sue.

Let's call this 1990's model "Thoroughly Modern Tillie"—she's the grandma of the old days, updated, in a new skin, with a new voice and a new confidence.

And there's a new one born every 10 minutes!

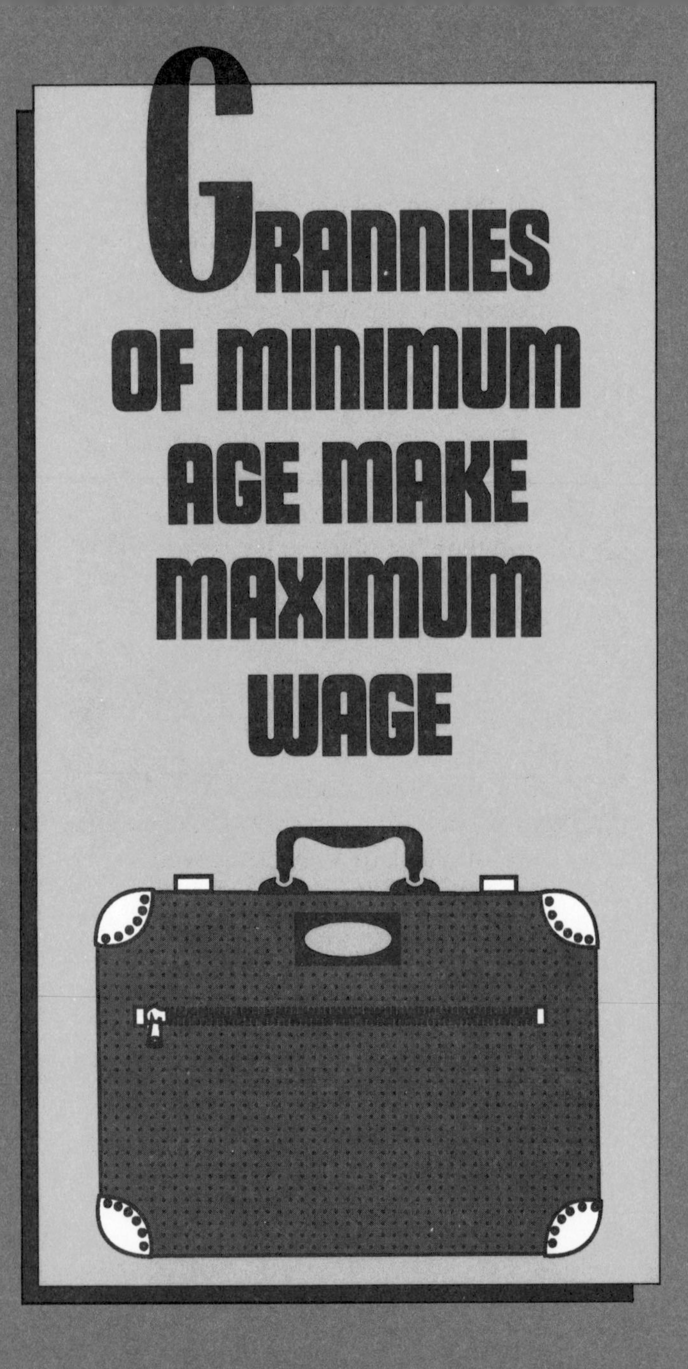
GRANNIES
OF MINIMUM
AGE MAKE
MAXIMUM
WAGE

GRANNIES OF MINIMUM AGE MAKE MAXIMUM WAGE

Grandma used to stay home to run the house. Now she's at the office running the company. Once she may have handled boredom—now she's handling the boardroom.

Grandma used to bake cookies and bread for the family; now, like the proverbial grandma **Sara Lee Lubin**, she may be baking bread and brownies for the whole country. Grandmas who sat bent over their treadle sewing machines making the family clothes have been replaced by grandmas like **Adele Fendi** and **Pauline Trigère** who have dressed the world in everything from jeans to sequins.

If grandma used to be an antique, now she's an antique dealer, like **Lillian Nassau**. Grandma used to stay home and polish the furniture; now, like grandma **Sys Cohen**, she polishes the lucite furniture she manufactures. Grandmas used to read us bedtime stories; now grandma **Ann McGovern** writes them.

Among the ranks of Grandmother Tycoons are the likes of **Joan Ganz Cooney**, also the grandmother of Big Bird and Sesame Street; Makeup Moguls **Estée Lauder** and **Mary Kay Ash**; and Motown's **Esther Edwards**, formerly the personal manager, and often unofficial Nana, of the teenaged Diana Ross, Stevie Wonder and Michael Jackson.

Executive grandmothers, no matter how busy, want to be grandmothers too. In fact, they insist on it. They make time for their grandchildren one way or another and then they make the amount of available time count.

Ellen Gordon, who works a 70-hour week running a 170-million-dollar company, says: *A grandparent's job is to give them lots of pleasure. To let them play in the sandbox with their party shoes. To let them have candy right before their dinner.* (Even easier done than said—for grandma **Ellen**'s the President of the Tootsie Roll Company . . . and, notice, please, how she's on the job plugging her product!)

I have a very busy life, myself, and in addition my children live far away, says children's writer **Ann McGovern**, author of more than 50 books. *I try to see them at least once a month, plus we take vacations with them. I'm not a grandma who bakes cookies or wears her hair in a bun. I decided my job is to provide the magic in their lives. I invent the role of grandma. When I'm with them it's all their time—we look at butterflies, we chase the waves and they think I'm made of magic and hugs.*

Grandma and TV writer/producer **Linda Kline**, whose granddaughter Robin Emily lives on a sheep farm, echoes this when she says, *I'm going to give this little Vermont granddaughter of mine a taste of New York and everything else life is. And no museums if she doesn't want to go! I'm planning Rumpelmayer's Tea Parties for her, dress-up parties with my friends' granddaughters (and with grandma too) and I want to bring music and the theater into her life.*

Grandma **Sys**, the furniture manufacturer, and her sister **Bernice** have nine granddaughters between them. *We have our own softball team, and the grandmas are players too, not just the umpires,* she says. *The kids come every weekend during the summer to "Camp Cohen." We swim, we have cookouts, we even tell ghost stories.*

Jean Rich, founder of Rich Airlines, which flew some of Malcolm Forbes' 70th Birthday Bash guests to Tangiers, makes free time to flit around Miami with her granddaughter Jenny. Similarly, says grandma **Rona G.**, *I may be a travel agent, but I make sure I'm here for my granddaughter, Samantha.* Samantha's so much a part of Rona's and her daughters' lives that she's known as *that baby with all the mothers.*

Motown's **Esther Edwards** says her granddaughters felt she had a tendency toward overkill when it came to offering them uplifting educational experiences. But she could always temper any excess by treating them to a Diana Ross event or the Wonder of Stevie himself. Things weren't working so well one afternoon when she dragged her granddaughter Robin to an event Robin herself did not consider important. *Grandma,* she said, in one of the most incredible role reversals in the ongoing relationship of the generations, *I hope you realize you're making me miss my soaps!*

In spite of the scarcity of time and the problems that distance often imposes, executive grannies are proud and pleased with the relationships they've developed.

Most feel they're much better grandparents than they were parents. *I was too busy with my career,* one says. *Not only that, when I was a mother I didn't have the money to spend on my kids and I didn't have the know-how, the confidence. Now I know I can walk into a restaurant, change a diaper and not be intimidated!* Or, says **Shirley L.**, *When my own kids were growing up, if the floor needed washing, I washed the floor. Now, the hell with the floor; I'd much rather play with my grandson.* From apparel executive **Doris B.**: *Last week I went on a hayride with my granddaughter Chloe. There I was, wearing $9,000 worth of Ralph Lauren and she's throwing hay all over me!*

Being a grandma is important in the lives of these women, but it's not the most important thing—it's an extra, a marvelous extra. They feel their role is to teach the things an older person, not a mother, can teach—and to make their grandchildren feel incredibly special and surrounded by love. Not a bad job, if you can get it!

YOUR GRANDMOTHER WEARS COMBAT BOOTS!

Yes, Virginia, there is a Grandma Corps. These days, grandmas can be found in the most surprising occupations—from standing around in combat boots to standing up doing comedy.

Rear Admiral **Grace Hopper** served in both the World War II WAVES and the Naval Reserves until she was retired aboard the USS Constitution in 1986. "Amazing Grace," with a PhD in mathematics, helped to write the computer language COBOL and to teach computers how to "think" in words. Colonel Grandma **Joan "Johnnie" Pantanelli** served in the Army Air Corps and today is an officer in the Civil Air Patrol. Grandmas now serve regularly in the Peace Corps, including, of course, **Lillian Carter**, and **Janet Klepper**, who at 74, having served two five-year stints in Guatemala, was brought back by popular (and her own) demand. The Peace Corps is actively recruiting senior citizens these days, a policy of its former director, grandma **Loret Ruppe**.

Grandmas like **Sandra Day O'Connor** are judges and they're lawyers, like grandma **Faith Seidenberg**, who successfully sued McSorley's Tavern in New York City for excluding women customers. Grandma **Ann Dwyer** is a 64-year-old kayaker, white-water rafter and tour guide. At the age of 80, **Elizabeth Terwilliger** conducts nature hikes and canoe trips six days a week through marshes, redwood forests, woodlands and mountains, teaching children on-site about the environment and its wonders.

Vivian Robbins, 61, is a psychiatric nurse and handywoman, who says, *I've always known how to do my own carpentry and electrical wiring, change the oil in my car, or the tires. Of course,* she allows, *my plumbing still needs a little work.*

Vita Gardner, 58, is the full-time band manager of The Coasters and has had granddaughter Monique, 5, on tour, on the set, and even on drums. Grandmas are also clowns; **Betty "Cozzie the Clown" Cozzens** is president and owner of Just Clowning

Around. Her company teaches clowning, offers clowns for hire, and is usually booked solid.

Grandmothers today are yogurt eaters and yoga teachers. They're even belly dancers. **Yvonne Redwine**, 53, of San Jose, is known as Farouché when she performs in her own nightclub called Sultana's. The **Sun Cities Pom Pom Girls**, a group of 16 cheerleaders ages 60-82, dance at sports arenas, churches and theaters across the country, and have appeared on the Johnny Carson Show.

More "Grancers": 84-year-old **Barbara Mosley** (with her 25-year-old partner Spenser) is a professional adagio dancer. **Barbara**, a 79-pound kewpie doll in tiny spangled costume, demonstrates extraordinary balance, timing and control as Spenser lifts, twists and tosses her through the air. **Dancing Grannies**, a 25-member dance troupe, do up to four miles of non-stop aerobic dancing while marching in parades. And **Dancers of the Third Age** is a Washington, D.C.-based company of 60-and-overs which has toured throughout the world. The oldest is **Thelma Tulane**, who took up modern dancing on her 80th birthday, which is surely one way to stay modern!

Barrie Bailey, a 73-year-old grandmother of four, leaps through windows and jumps off bridges as a Hollywood stuntwoman. She's also managed to leap into seven marriages (eight, if you count the one man she married twice). *I guess,* says **Barrie**, *I'm just always a bride and never a bridesmaid.*

While **Barrie** obviously spends a lot of time wearing the dress her kids call her "wash'n'wear wedding dress," and while other modern grandmas wear combat boots, some wear little or nothing at all. **Leola Harlow** started a brand-new career as a professional stripper at the age of 81. And, for a senior citizens pinup calendar, 62-year-old **Martha West** posed nude, except for a strategically placed floppy purple hat and a glass of champagne.

And finally, grandmas are even stand-up comedians. Grandma **Merrilyn Belgum**, 65, retired after 40 years as a social worker to become a full-time comic. *Raising six children to adulthood makes you REAL funny,* she says. The only thing she won't make fun of is *double chins or [our] appearances as we grow older.*

What do grandmothers so diverse have in common? Scratch the surface and you'll discover a universal and unconditional love affair with their grandchildren. Trite as it sounds, each reports some unique version of instant and overwhelming love. Recent grandmother **Mary Travers**, the female voice of folksingers Peter, Paul, and Mary, says, *All through the sixties people kept talking about free love, but I never found any myself. Finally I discovered what it is—it's being a grandmother! Love without responsibility or guilt! You get to be excessive and spoil them—and it's not your problem!*

Other grandmothers—maybe not as famous but equally as vocal and exactly on key—say, *Just when you think you'd loved just about everyone who could possibly be important in your life, along comes this brand new, unbelievably important new person.* AND *Everybody tells you about it, but nobody can explain how it gets under your skin. You hear about it but you can't know it until you go through it.* AND *It's a chance to have all the wonder and magic you have with your own children, but without the anxiety and questioning "Am I doing it right?" They're just there for you to love and encourage and you're there to give them something special.*

AND *It's so much better than being a mother.* AND *It totally jiggles you. Suddenly you can't imagine life without this child, just like you can't imagine life without YOUR children.* AND *I don't know what we're going to do if this baby gets any cuter—I think we'll all burst!* AND *Everybody always said it's so great. I said, I'm not the type—How great can it be? After all, it's just a baby. But, it's just so exciting! You can sit and watch this baby just BE—It's better than any Broadway show or any TV. You just sit there and watch—Look! She's breathing! Her nostrils are opening! Her eyelids work! . . .*

THERE'LL BE
A HOT TIME
IN THE
OLD GOWN
TONIGHT!

THERE'LL BE A HOT TIME IN THE OLD GOWN TONIGHT!

The 1990's grandma is often single. She's lively and enthusiastic. She's eager to expand her life and to share it with someone. But single men, especially in her age group, are scarcer these days than hen's teeth, mink bikinis, and male pregnancies. One grandma, almost svelte after months at NutraSystem, bemoaning her eternal diet and seemingly endless single status, joked, *I'm getting a great figure, but I'm getting it for the worms!* This particular Thoroughly Modern Tillie (TMT) told her granddaughter that she was considering taking up embalming just to get next to an (almost) warm body. Her granddaughter, who is definitely a Thoroughly Modern Filly (TMF), suggested that she get "hip to the program" and try something a little more modern than the church supper to connect with a fellow antique.

What follows are some Personals ads written one giggly afternoon by this TMT (who wishes to remain anonymous until the results are in) with the help of her granddaughter, TMF.

GOT-IT-ALL GRANNY seeking sprightly old geezer for Disco, not Desk-o, Bongos, not Bingo.
(ATHLETIC, Yes! ARTHRITIC, No!)

GRANDMA, not too used, but easily amused wants to be cruised, and possibly fused.
(RUNNERS, Yes! RHEUMATOIDS, No!)

HEALTHY, ACTIVE GRANDFATHER WANTED for vegetarian grandmother who still sneaks a hunk of meat once in a while.
(CONTINENTAL, Yes!
INCONTINENT, No!)

KNOCKOUT GRANDMOTHER, seeking Big Ole Bruiser in Boxers, who thinks he can still go 10 rounds.
(ARROGANCE, Yes! FLATULENCE, No!)

WIDOW-WOMAN, PACKS A MEAN BOX LUNCH. Yep, my pore Judd is daid—if you've still got some fringe on top, you can take me out in your surrey—or your Benz.
(CHARIOTS, Yes! WHEELCHAIRS, No!)

O CAPTAIN, MY CAPTAIN! ARE YOU LOST AT SEA? Sometime Second Mate, on even keel, not broad of beam, is searching all shores. Sound your SOS and we'll sail off into the sunset.
(HOT POTATO, Yes!
COUCH POTATO, No!)

MARE, NOT SO GRAY, NOT SO OLD, still frisky, fair, and hot-to-trot, wants salt-and-pepper palomino or Italian stallion not yet ready to be put out to pasture.
(IMPORTANT, Yes! IMPOTENT, No!)

IT AIN'T KANSAS AND I AIN'T AUNTIE EM! Not-So-Wicked Witch awaits weal wizard to fowwow the yewwow bwick woad. Pwease, no Cowardly Wions, Tin Men or Scare Cwows.
(PACESETTER, Yes! PACEMAKER, No!)

HEY, KING CHARMING! CINDERELLA'S GRAN awaits you with perfect pumpkin pie. Bring size 7½ Reebok for perfect fit.
(CEO, Yes! CPR, No!)

SPRY GRANDMOTHER LOOKING FOR MAY-TO-DECEMBER RELATIONSHIP—May we both be here next December!
(DEPENDABLE, Yes! DEPENDS, No!)

And this is the ad they actually ran:

REMARKABLE WIDOW, 54, winsome, wise and witty, wants bachelor 50-70, who can describe himself WITHOUT mentioning his possessions (but has them . . .).

SEX CHANGES

It's a different sexual world out there for the thoroughly modern (often single) grandmother—and this sometimes has an impact on her grandchildren too.

John W. reports that his single grandma, **Jackie**, sure doesn't sit home reading large print books. She's actually started dating. Recently she called him and said, *It's 40 years since I dated anyone . . . I don't know what to do with a man. Above the waist? Below the waist? Of course, what makes it even harder is—what used to be above my waist is now below my waist.*

Tommy C. tells of being at the awkward yet raging hormonal age of 13 and walking in, unannounced and unheard, on his grandmother making very explicit sexual advances upon his grandfather's person. *Well,* he thought, *If she can do it, I guess I certainly can!* This incident changed his entire sexual outlook, he says. And Linda R. says that her grandmother was the first person she told about her "First Time." *I'm not sure why. She's such a big part of my life and I knew she'd get a kick out of being included.*

Grandmas today don't just sit around playing tame games of bridge. In California, a group of middle-aged moms and grandmoms calling themselves the **Kensington Ladies Erotica Society** met monthly for years sharing their most sizzling sexual fantasies. Eventually they wrote them up and got them published in a slick little paperback entitled **Ladies' Home Erotica**. It became a best-seller!

At a Senior Citizens conference, an expert in the field of human sexuality was speaking about options and choices for single women. Among the things she mentioned was an inexpensive vibrator put out by Hitachi. At that point a hand shot up and an obviously upset grandmother hoisted herself out of her seat. *Uh, oh,* thought the speaker, *here comes the morality lecture.* The question, however, was, *How do you spell Hitachi?*

And just in case we didn't know that grannies today do more under the sheets than smooth them down, Golden Girl and grandma **Estelle Getty** says, *Old people do have sex and they have it a lot. They're just doing it a little more slowly, which, come to think of it, is not a bad thing.* And they SHOULD be having sex more. After all, *It's not like anyone's going to get pregnant.*

Goodness Gracious,
Great Gram's a Flyer!

GOODNESS GRACIOUS, GREAT GRAM'S A FLYER!

And, guess what else? GOOD GOLLY MS. MOLLY'S A DIVER! And that's just the tippy top of the iceberg of amazing hobbies and interests grandmas are pursuing today.

Faith Seidenberg signed up for flying lessons at the age of 62 and now flies almost every day. Grandma **Faith** says, *I'm not living the last third of my life as if it's already over. People live their lives as if the first two-thirds were all there is.* She's flown granddaughter Rachel, 13, to Montreal for the weekend and is encouraging Rachel's own flying lessons. She also loves to travel the world. Her granddaughter is a most willing companion and the beneficiary of a Kenya safari and an ecology trek to the Galapagos. When Rachel heard that her grandmother would be going solo on an Egyptian cruise, she said, *Grandma, you brat, how could you go without me?*

Ann McGovern is a Scuba Diving Grandma.

Her grandchildren are champing at their regulators till they're 12 and old enough to join her; meanwhile they have to be content with snorkeling. **Leslie Dessauer** is a Greased Lightning Grandma; she still regularly tears up the asphalt on her Harley. She's biked cross country four times and would love to do it someday with her grandsons, now both under two, but says, *I may have to hit the rocking chair before they hit the road.*

Hulda Crooks, 92 years old, has climbed Mt. Whitney 22 times and was nicknamed "Grandma Fuji" after her most recent triumph. **Bess James** of San Jacinto, California, is a 79-year-old marathon runner who carried the Olympic Torch in 1984 through Santa Fe and has a 10K race named after her. Grandmother **Jacque Proctor** cycled 20,000 miles across four continents at the age of 62 with emphysema and only 55% use of her lungs. And 79-year-old **Arda Perkins** is a blind race-walker who plans to participate in the National Senior Olympics. *I bring up the rear. I don't care about winning a medal. I love the excitement and the people.*

Grandma may also be a parachutist, a discus thrower, or a skier. But don't make the mistake of assuming that our Thoroughly Modern Momma is all brawn and no brains—in fact, she's been broadening herself in all areas, except, of course, the beam.

Just about the time her grandson starts trudging off to first grade, she's apt to be backing her Honda into some school. Whether it's art or computers, sociology or Spanish, she's serious and successful. Like **Sarah Wilford**, who returned to school in psychology and now teaches, consults, writes and heads Sarah Lawrence's Early Childhood Program. Like pleasingly plump **Dottie Thompson**, 67, who enrolled at Cerritos College and was elected Homecoming Queen by the entire student body, beating out six terrific young twigs of 20. To say nothing of Grandma **Libby Klar**, who got her BA with honors in history at 68, and says, *My young classmates treated me as just another student . . . Age was usually irrelevant, although I must admit to hearing audible gasps when I made some firsthand observations on the Great Depression.*

Today's grandma propels herself into these exciting new activities with a jolt of confidence from the previous successes in her life. But she also gets an added boost from the sudden recognition of her brilliance that comes when her children have children:

I can't believe how smart I got to be the minute my son had a child, says **Ellen A.** *She's a lot more understanding about who I am now that she's a parent,* comments **Barbara K.** The ultimate Dawning of the Light Story comes from **Shirley L.**:

When my daughter Gabrielle was a little girl, one time it rained for maybe three weeks straight. I was stuck home the whole time with my three kids. I wanted to kill them all, but instead I picked up her rocking chair and I threw it against the wall. From that time on, she always reminded me, "You broke my rocking chair." One day when Damian, my grandson, was four, it was a horrible rainy day. At around 5 o'clock, Gaby walked into my kitchen and said to me, "Mom, I got it about the rocking chair—forget the whole thing!"

GRANNY, GET YOUR GUN!

When granny feels strongly about something these days, she doesn't sit on the sidelines—she does something about it. In fact, another reason grandma doesn't HAVE a lap to sit on these days may be that she's out DOING laps: she's crusading for the causes that matter to her. Her reasons were best expressed by grandmother **Lady Bird Johnson** when she said, *I want to pay my rent on the world.*

Grandmas today have a sense of their own power. Working through seniors groups, they've fought to repeal the 1988 Medicare Catastrophic Coverage Act with its unpopular surtax.

In 1982, **Barbara Wiedner** founded Grandmothers for Peace to do what she could to secure and protect her grandchildren's futures. The organization has expanded from the 11 original members to over 20,000 members in some 30 nations. And grandmothers were among those who walked almost clear across the USA from Los Angeles to Washington, D.C. in an

8-month peace march.

In Argentina, The Abuelas are a group of grandmothers who organized, despite a violent repressive regime, to locate children and grandchildren who had been kidnapped as subversives by the 1976 military junta. Some 39 of these "disappeared ones" have been located and restored; hundreds remain missing. And grandmothers in Glen Cove, New York, now patrol their housing project to prevent crack sales from taking place.

Grandmothers have joined daughters and granddaughters on both sides of the abortion issue. Many appeared at the April, 1989 Abortion March; one family marched with a huge banner boldly proclaiming "Four Generations for Choice and Equality."

And in an operation known as the Granny Sting, **Muriel Clark**, 82, a retired social worker and activist, posed as a potential nursing home applicant. Teamed with an undercover cop pretending to be her son, she "wore a wire" and assumed a false identity attempting to smoke out illicit payoffs. Bribes totaling $55,000 were offered to her, and this eventually resulted in two indictments and a shakeup of the whole nursing home industry.

Other grandmothers, of course, help the homeless, read to the blind, are Foster Grandparents, volunteer at nursing homes, day care centers and hospitals, work in their churches and temples, and devote their time to and raise funds for causes of every description.

If grandmas are feisty, active, and sure of themselves these days, it's because women of this generation have achieved enormous personal advances. They won't be taken advantage of or be denied anything they think they deserve. Connecticut grandmother and music teacher **Catherine Pollard** took on the Boy Scouts of America, who refused to allow her to be a Scoutmaster, until they eventually cried "Uncle!" (or "Aunt!" as the case may be). Grandma **Dotty S.** reports actually socking a guard who got surly with her at a New York Knicks basketball game. (He needed 20 stitches.) Would she do it again? *Definitely . . . but next time, I'd have him remove his eyeglasses first . . .*

Grand-
mother,
What
Big
Thighs
You
Have!

GRANDMOTHER, WHAT BIG THIGHS YOU HAVE!

You wouldn't hear Red Riding Hood saying that to her grandma these days. If Red Riding Hood were to come tripping through the woods today, she'd most likely meet her grandmother aerobically bounding through it herself. Granny'd be working on shedding that cellulite, she'd be shimmying and shaking those saddlebags, and slashing that dress size down to somewhere south of a 6.

In fact the chances of Red Riding Hood even looking for her grandma at home in bed are pretty slim, for grandma's hard at work getting slim. For every grandma like **Joy M.**, who doesn't exercise, saying, *If you don't jiggle it around too much, don't use it too much, it'll last a whole lot longer,* there are 10 like **Carol B.**, who says, *I joined a gym when I realized if I didn't do something soon, one morning I'd find my whole body lying in one big flesh puddle around my feet. I bought leotards and I even wear them, but I swear, if Jane Fonda becomes a grandmother, I'll have to quit. I'll take to a wheelchair and throw a* *big quilt over myself!* Grandma **Mary S.**, who now works out religiously, says, *The backs of my arms were so bad I knew with a strong backhand I could flab someone to death.*

Grandmas keep in shape doing aerobic dancing with Richard Simmons on his Silver Foxes videotape. *(Richard Simmons, cute little boy that he is, I'd like to send him to Alice Crimmins,* grunts one disgruntled granny, *and I'm not so fonda Jane, either.)* And they're also firming up on tape with grandma **Angela Lansbury** of "Murder She Wrote" fame. *("Firmer Old Stoat"* they should call this tape, suggests another Grand Wit.)

Some grandmothers take their fitness so seriously that the spare room they used to devote solely to grandchildren's visits now looks like a Nursery à la Nautilus; it's treadmills and teddy bears, rowing machines and "Row, Row, Row Your Boat." Today's grandma is chinning as she's wiping chins, sweating as she's "sweetie"-ing.

The 1990's grandma not only works out to stay fit, she eats healthier and better to stay trim. And it all started with Grandma **Jean Nidetch**, who founded Weight Watchers out of her apartment in the early sixties. Now there are thousands of Weight Watchers franchises operating all over the world.

Joan B., trim and tight at 54, remarks, *Our bodies have to last a whole lot longer than our grandmothers' did. And I take mine to lots more places and dress it a whole lot sexier.*

She's right. Grannies today are slithering in teddies, not slurping down toddies. Sometimes their outrageousness shocks the kids. Grandma **Anita R.** asked her son Richard to help her pick out a sexy, unfrumpy bathing suit for her new Florida lifestyle. He was horrified at her spangled selections, so he showed her a more demure model complete with attached skirt. To this **Anita** responded, *I'm going to a condo, not a convent.* Said another daughter to her mother, regarding her attire, *When are you going to start acting like a grandmother?* Her 62-year-old mother replied, *I don't have to act like a grandmother. I* am *one.*

WEIGHTY GRANNECDOTES

Grandma **Dorothy S**. to her medical student grandson Bob: *When I'm doing my aerobics I get short of breath—couldn't you install a pulsemaker?*

Jeff K. was at a restaurant with his grandmother, **Marcia**. Hearing her order a steak, Jeff said, *Come on Grams, red meat's not good for you.* **Marcia** shot back instantly: *Now, honey, don't be a nag—I ordered it well done.*

Grandmothers are like chicken soup, says grandma **Joan B**. *They're delicious and they make you feel good . . . And you can have extra portions without gaining an ounce.*

And speaking of weighty matters, here is an ancient adage that has been handed down in virtually every known language and culture, from grandmother to granddaughter:

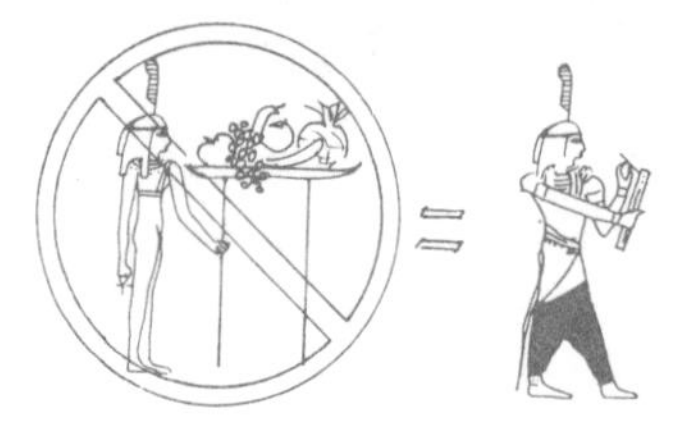

Hieroglyphics

腹は 八分目

Japanese

Al tochal baamidah—yihyu lecha raglayim shmenot.

Hebrew

Ne mange pas debout—tes jambes grossiront.

French

Non mangiare in piedi—sennò le gambe ti diventeranno grossissime.

Italian

Don't eat standing up—you'll get fat legs.

English

THE OTHER WOMAN

I don't think he's sent her flowers—yet—and he probably doesn't remember her birthday any more than he remembers mine, but I think he spends Thursdays with her and last week I think it was Friday too. I'm not normally a jealous person, but this is almost more than I can stand. I can't bear the thought that he loves HER more than me . . .

Sound familiar? It's a classic example of The Other Woman. With the possible exception of Eve (who seems to have had no competitor available to worry about) women have been putting up with The Other Woman since the dawn of recorded history.

Alas, even if you're a 1990's Grandmother, you're no exception. Worse, you know exactly who your competition is—it's THE OTHER GRANDMOTHER. For there almost always is one. In fact, in this age of Spouse Shuffling and Relative Recycling, sometimes there are even two!

If you're one of the lucky ones, The Other Woman is G.N.A.P. (Geographically Not A

Problem); she lives far enough away not to pose a major threat. If you're among the not-so-lucky, winning this competition can definitely be a problem. (If you're the mother of the mother of the child, you have less of a problem. In that case, you're probably THE Grandmother. If you're the mother of the father, your only hope may be to rush out, adopt a grown daughter and hope she gets pregnant soon.)

Some strategies will simply not ensure your being the favorite. A face lift will do no good. And neither will a sexy new outfit—unless you're willing to try a Teenage Mutant Ninja Turtle costume. (Do not be cavalier and discard this idea—it may yet be your best bet.)

Other alternatives: You can locate the perfect retirement home for the O.W.—in Namibia. You can recommend she give HIM apples and dates for Trick or Treat . . . Suggest she give HIM the Encyclopedia Britannica for Christmas . . . Give her chamber music tickets and suggest she take HIM . . . Share with her the liver recipe he loved so much last time he visited you . . . Give her all your frequent flyer points—with a one-way ticket . . . Give her sky-diving lessons . . . Get her a night job . . . Enroll her in the Peace Corps . . . Anonymously submit her name for jury duty and pray she gets a treason case . . . If you're willing to pull out all the stops, you can always introduce her to YOUR boyfriend, and hope they hit it off.

If you draw the line short of these suggestions, you may have to give up, grin and bear it, and hope this strategy does not create any more wrinkles than you already have.

And speaking of wrinkles, that brings up The O.O.W.—The Other Other Woman in your life. She's the one that's most surprising because, though you live with her every day, somehow it's always a shock when she turns up. She's the one you find peering back at you from inside the mirror. You know that deep down you really feel 32, and you're doing all the things that younger women used to do. So who *is* this older person staring back at you?

There's only one solution to the problem of The Other Other Woman, says grandma **Mimi G.:** *After a certain age, there's only one* *way to deal with the mirror. YOU LOOK ONLY AT YOUR LIPS! LIPS DO NOT CHANGE. (All right, maybe they change a little, but not nearly as much as the rest of you, so just focus on the center and stay clear of the edges.) EVERY ONCE IN A WHILE, IF YOU'RE FEELING REALLY GOOD, YOU CAN SNEAK A QUICK LOOK UP AT AN EYE, A CHEEK, AN EARRING. BUT ONLY IF YOU'RE FEELING REALLY GREAT AND IF YOU DO IT REALLY FAST. OTHERWISE, JUST THE LIPS!* In this way you do away with The Other Other Woman and can always maintain your perfect psychological age—be it 16 or 36.

THE "GRAMMIE" AWARDS

Here are proposed annual "Grammies" which celebrate separate areas of Grandmotherly Achievement. Each is named after (but certainly not sponsored by) a major corporation.

THE PLAYSKOOL GRAMMIE: to be awarded each year to the grandmother who proves that any household object can function as an interesting toy or learning experience. This year the award goes to **Ellie S**. for opening wide the doors of her priceless Steuben Glass cabinet to granddaughter Emily. (Unfortunately, this will disqualify **Ellie** for next year's Bandaid Grammie Award for Safety.)

THE EASTMAN KODAK GRAMMIE: to be awarded each year to the grandmother who demonstrates the most profligate use of film. This year a second award to **Ellie S.**, who submitted upwards of 10,000 candids of her second granddaughter, 3-month-old Danielle.

THE LIBERTY TRAVEL GRAMMIE: awarded each year to the most unusual trip planned by a grandmother for her grandchild. To be shared jointly this year by **Linda K.** and her friend **Nancy D.**, who actually booked passage on the Q.E.II in the year 2004 for their six-week-old granddaughters Robin and Ariel.

THE NIKE GOOD SPORT GRAMMIE: to be awarded annually to the grandmother who shows herself to be a good sport in the face of adversity. Awarded this year to **Phyllis H.** who, grandchildless and faced constantly with her many grandmother friends' incessant bragging and snapshots, began whipping out photographs of HER new grandchild—her daughter's horse Sally.

THE PLANNED PARENTHOOD SAFE SEX GRAMMIE: awarded to the grandmother who best demonstrates to her grandchild that these days you take your life in your loins. To **Karen B.**, who gave her grandson Eric a box of condoms before he went off to college, along with the following poem:

Don't think I'm a nag
Or a terrible drag
As you go off to school
All filled up with fuel
If you must be a stag
Stick these on your flag!

Love, Grams

THE TRUMP SHUTTLE GRAMMIE: awarded annually to that grandmother who puts the shuttle to its best or most conspicuous—à la Donald—use. This year to **Ann McG.**, who, speaking to her 5-year-old grandson Chris on the evening of her return from a visit with him in Maryland, asked him why he was crying. *Because I want to see you, Grandma,* he said. *When?* she asked. *Right now,* he said. Whereupon she picked up her bag and grabbed the next shuttle back to Washington.

Anything
You Can Say,
I Can Say
Better!

ANYTHING YOU CAN SAY, I CAN SAY BETTER!

Thoroughly Modern Tillie (TMT), a savvy, with-it grandmother, says, *If something's worth saying, I can say it better.* So we tossed her some well-known, well-said quotes from some well-known people. They are printed below, followed by Tillie's corrections, corollaries and clarifications.

Beware: Tillie is apt to be irreverent, but never irrelevant. We wouldn't dare argue with her—everybody knows any grandmother worth her garlic repeats on you.

There will be some men who under no circumstances can allow a woman to pay a check. By all means, allow him to pay for his own outdated view of chivalry.

Dee Wedemeyer

. . . And besides, you can put the money toward a face lift.

Thoroughly Modern Tillie (TMT)

A grandmother is a woman who used to sit up with her children and now sits up with her children's children.

Unknown

. . . Unless she has a hot date.

TMT

The grandmother of today has something that the grandmother of the past didn't have—blonde hair.

Unknown

. . . Vidal, what did I tell you about tattling?

TMT

A stitch in time would have confused Einstein.

Unknown

. . . Come right over, honey, I'll sew it for you.

TMT

If a man has nothing to eat, fasting is the most intelligent thing he can do.

Herman Hesse

. . . Wrong. A man is never more than a block away from a McDonald's.

TMT

The reverse side also has a reverse side.

Japanese Proverb

. . . I can think of nothing more depressing than having two reverse sides!

TMT

We are all born charming, fresh, and spontaneous and must be civilized before we are fit to participate in society.

Miss Manners (Judith Martin)

. . . That's a mommy's job. Now let's get back to our food fight.

TMT

Men are creatures with two legs and eight hands.

Jayne Mansfield

. . . Until you marry them.

TMT

No [I don't understand my husband's theory of relativity], but I know my husband and I know he can be trusted.

Elsa Einstein

. . . I beg to differ, dearie, but my theory is: a husband can only be trusted around his relatives.

TMT

How old would you be if you didn't know how old you was?

Satchel Paige

. . . With makeup, eighteen; without is another story entirely.

TMT

If you want a place in the sun, prepare to put up with a few blisters.

Abigail Van Buren

. . . Not at my house; I have Number 29 Sun Block.

TMT

The difference between genius and stupidity is that genius has its limits.

Unknown

. . . Except, of course, for my grandson, Sheldon.

TMT

Happiness is seeing Lubbock, Texas, in the rearview mirror.

Song Title

. . . Happiness is seeing your granddaughter in the dancing school mirror.

TMT

I don't know the key to success but the key to failure is trying to please everybody.

Bill Cosby

. . . Except if you have my recipe for apple pie.

TMT

Don't think: Look!

Wittgenstein

. . . Don't look: Eat!

TMT

If I had my life to live over, I'd live over a delicatessen.

Unknown

. . . If I had my life to live over, I'd only have grandchildren.

TMT

It is easier to get forgiveness than permission.

Murphy's Law, Book Two

. . . Go, angelface, and have a good time.

TMT

Never lend your car to anyone to whom you have given birth.

Erma Bombeck

. . . Use mine, sweetheart, your mother never did learn how to share!

TMT

Women who miscalculate are called "mothers."

Abigail Van Buren

. . . I told her to study her math, but she was too busy on the telephone.

TMT

No matter how old a mother is, she watches her middle-aged children for signs of improvement.

Florida Scott-Maxwell

. . . No matter how old a grandmother is, she knows her grandchildren are perfect exactly as they are.

TMT

YOU'RE A GRAND OLD BAG!
In Grandchildren's Own Words

It's very clear that the 1990's Grandmother is a class act in every way. So it's not so surprising she gets rave reviews from her biggest fans. Here's what some grand-children have to say:

My grandma always gives me advice on my life. She is the most precious human in the world.

Juliana R., age 15

I told my mother, "You had Grandma your whole life. It's my turn now."

Rebecca L., age 8

Sometimes she is so alive with spirit she'll do just about anything you do.

Evins S., age 12

I finally admitted to my Gram that when my brother and I were a lot younger, we'd always go into this closet she had and eat the candy in there. She said, "Sweetheart, who exactly do you think was replenishing the candy in the closet so you and your brother could heist it in the first place!"

Mara K., age 13

She has such a loving, soft heart. She thinks of everyone else and then herself. She is so kind and special. She understands that I'm a teenager and I like to go out so she gives me money and hopes I have a good time (and she means it).

Melinda A., age 15

I was telling my grandmother about school, about how I was editor of the newspaper, president of my class, and my grades were mostly good but I'd just flunked a math test and knew it would freak my dad out, so I didn't want to call him. "Fax him if he can't take a joke," she said.

Ken K., age 20

She says, “Touch with your eyes and look with your hands.” I don’t really get it, but it sounds cool.

Shirley M., age 13

My granny lets me lick the cake mixture when she is finished. She lets me leave my food, and she spoils me so much that when I grow up I won’t want anything.

Sandra W., age 10

Everything she does means a lot to me. The most important thing she usually tells me is I love you. Which parents usually forget.

R.M.R., age 14

My grandmother’s the greatest. My mom was pissed off when I got my ears pierced, but my grandmother gave me all her leftovers.

Kevin G., age 18

Nana's littlest fans have more to add. They were asked: If Grandma were an animal what would she be? Here come the (unexpurgated and uncorrected) answers—straight from the colts' mouths:

She would be a turtle because she takes her time off to make me happy.

Hannah B., age 9

A parrot becuase she talks alot.

Nestor N., age 10

A cat she is so loveable.

Alexander S., age 10

A beutiful goldfish because I love goldfish and you talk to them about your problems.

Rose D., age 8

A dolphin because I can swim with her

Mary V., age 8

I would like her to be my on little fluffy nice cat

Thamar H., age 8

A parakeet. So I could talk to her.

Adrienne N., age 8

A hamster. So I could keep my grandmother.

Dierdre T., age 10

A lepard. Because I like leperds.

Laura O., age 8

Bear. A bear that protects her cubs.

Jessica, age 7

Bird. Because she has a nice voys.

Michelle S., age 7

A hippoppatamus. Cause she's chubby.

Bruce C., age 7

A cute little pudle. Because she's as sweet as one and she is a bautiful person.

Krista L., age 8

They call her by many names—Grandma and Nana; Gram and Yaya and Mamma; Nonna and Abuela; Inang, Ammachi and more. But whatever they call her, these littlest fans all agree that the best thing she ever said to them was, *I love you.*

AND WE LOVE YOU TOO, GRANDMA!